To my son _____

To my daughter _____

who was born __/___/_____

in city of _____

The 9 months Diary of your life

before your birth

Hi Mom,

I'm here, right here inside of you.

I am just 4 weeks old and very tiny and about the size a poppy seed.

Right now your body is performing a miracle. You are creating a new person, me, your baby and in only 9 months you will be able to see me and to hold me in your arms.

Where I am now it's warm and cozy. Your body is the whole universe for me and I find it very comforting.

I can feel your love for me growing stronger with every passing day.

I want you to be happy in this experience, because I can feel your emotions.

My brain is beginning to form and it is up to you how smart I will be. Try to avoid cigarette's smoke and alcohol, do not be nervous. Stay away from drinking strong coffee and soda.

Always eat well and make sure you get plenty of sleep. Look at beautiful things, think beautiful thoughts, and think of me and keep a positive attitude.

Talk to me when we are alone. Even though I cannot hear your voice, I can receive your feelings and emotions, and I do need your love, more than you will ever know.

Right now my heart is represented by a microscopic tube, but already it has begun to fight for life.

I am so excited becoming a human being.

I love you Mom

Hi baby

Hi Mom,

I am about the size of a sesame seed, and I look more like a tiny tadpole than a human.

Are you sure I am not a frog, Mom? Just making you smile.   OK, I will try another way - My small body is bent in the form of the letter "C". Feel better?

It is possible already to see where my legs, my hands and my head will be.

Even now my tiny heart has formed and waiting for love.

And my "BIG" tiny heart is   full of love for you Mom.

I love you Mom

Hi baby

Week 6

Hi Mom,

My Heart Belongs to You!
The first heartbeats have begun! Now I am an embryo.

My nose, mouth,and ears are beginning to take shape. They will be ready for kissing in eight months.

There are Visual vials on my head – my future eyes, nostrils and an opening for the mouth. They are starting to form.

My tiny heart is beating about 100 to 150 times a minute.
Almost twice as fast as yours and blood is beginning to course through my tiny body.

My intestines are developing and my lungs have appeared.

My glands are forming, as is the rest of my brain, my muscles, and my bones.

Right now, I am about the size of a lentil.

I love you Mom

Hi baby

Week 7

Hi Mom,

I'm tiny (about the size of a blueberry) but gaining fast!

Do you know I have a small tail on my body? Are you sure I am a human being? Not a monkey?
Just joking, I wanted to feel you smile.

The tail will disappear within a few weeks, but that's the only thing getting smaller.

Good news - I have doubled in size since last week and I got my first organ feelings –Vestibular mechanism.

My skin has sensitivity.
I can feel a tiny tongue in my mouth. My hands and feet are emerging from developing arms and legs — although they look more like something you paddle a boat with at this point.

I love you Mom

Hi baby

Hi Mom, I am swimming!

I am about the size of a kidney bean and there is some changing in my body. Good news - my "tail" is just about gone.

Thank God I am not a monkey :)

My eyelids practically cover my eyes. My beautiful eyes :) My lungs are developing.

Already there has appeared a liquid in your belly in which I must live until my birthday. This is my own ocean. Such a good feeling. There is nothing more enjoyable than swimming warmly, happily and safely inside of your belly. And this is a good exercises. Good start to be an Olympic swimming champion :)

I now can feel pain. I guess part of being a human is being able to feel pain.

I have begun to feel my first movements. My palms have become sensitive. These feelings are amazing.

I can touch and feel my own body and the cord that connect us together. Let's try an experiment, try to touch your belly, and I will try to touch it also from my side. So we can get to know each other better until I am born.

I love you Mom

Hi baby

Week 9

Hi Mom,

Now I am about the size of a grape. Anyway, I am starting to look more and more human.

My eyes are fully formed, but my eyelids are shut and have not opened yet.

Also I now have tiny earlobes, my mouth, my nose, and my nostrils are more distinct.

My heart has now divided into four chambers, and the valves are beginning to form.
My organs, muscles, and nerves are almost formed.

The external sex organs are there but won't be distinguishable as boy or girl for another few weeks.

I do not know what I want to be - a boy or a girl. What about you Mom, what do you want a boy or a girl?

I love you Mom

Hi baby

Week 10

Hi Mom,

As you know Mom, I am getting bigger every day. Now I am about the size of a kumquat . Do you realize we have now completed the most critical portion of my development.

My vital organs — including my brain, intestines, kidneys and liver are in place and starting to function, though they are still developing.

My nails are starting to form on my fingers and toes. They are so tiny.   There is this peach-fuzz hair beginning to grow on my tender skin.

My limbs can bend now.

There is more - the outline of my spine is clearly visible through my thin skin, and my spinal nerves are beginning to stretch out from my spinal cord.

What a wonderful change this is that's taking place.

My forehead is temporarily bulging as my brain is developing. My head now measures about half the length of my body, but even this doesn't spoil my beauty:)

I love you Mom

Hi baby

Week 11

Hi Mom,

Now I look like a fig and I'm almost fully formed.

In a few months I will look like you Mom.... or like Dad.

Soon my tiny hands will open and close into fists. Such tiny fists. So tiny. But they will grow.

I am already trying to kick and stretch but my movements are still very confined.

I am glad I cannot hurt you with my kicking . These movements will soon become more frequent as my body grows and I become stronger. Soon you will begin to feel my acrobatics, just wait another month or two.

I promise you I will be as gentle as I can.

I love you Mom

Hi baby

Week 12

Hi Mom

My size almost has doubled in the last three weeks! I am about the size of a lime. And my brain is developing more and more every day. Now it looks very similar to the brain of an adult, but only in a miniature size.

My liver is already starting to develop bile. Isn't it amazing? My skeleton is formed. The fingers on my hands and the toes on my feet are now divided, and the nails are continuing to grow.

My face is beginning to look human: my eye muscles will clench, and my mouth will make sucking movements.

Already my tiny stomach is capable of pushing through food.

It can now actively absorb glucose and sugar. I like the taste of sugar.

Great news, Mom - the time has come to define which sex I will be. I will cross my tiny fingers to be a boy...Or a girl ... Or twins... Or triplets ....OK, time to stop joking.

I hope you will be satisfied with me whether I am a boy or a girl.

Anyway it is too late to make any changes now.

I love you Mom

Hi baby

Week 13

Hi Mom,

I now have my own individual identification ID :) Really. My fingerprints have formed on my tiny fingertips. It's amazing isn't it?

My vocal cords are beginning to form – Someday, perhaps I can be an American Idol :) Why not?
Anything is possible in your world, Mom.

My face is beginning to look more and more human every day. I hope it will be a beautiful or a handsome face.

My veins and organs are clearly visible through my still-thin skin, and my body is starting to catch up with my head — which makes up just a third of my body size now.   I am about a size of a medium shrimp.

My body has already developed twenty milk teeth in my mouth. Excellent teeth. Hollywood's smile.   My pancreas is beginning to produce insulin so from now on I can try a sugar. Joke.

I love you Mom

Hi baby

Week 14

Hi Mom,

I am about the size of a lemon.

My hands and feet are more flexible and active now. But they are still so tiny. Who knows maybe Someday I will be a sprinter. An Olympic sprinter. Or dancer... Or ... Who knows.

I can now squint, frown, grimace. Maybe I will be an actor?... Or actress?... OK, just a movie star.

I am stretching out.

My kidneys are now producing urine, which I releases into the water around me. But do not worry. It is clean and sterile here where I am, because my little ocean changes the water about 10 times a day.

I can tell you Mom, your body is working so wonderfully well.

Great news: I can now suck my thumb! It is an amazing feeling and I like it. It make me feel calm and cozy.

I love you Mom

Hi baby

Hi Mom,

I now am about the size of an apple.

Now air sacs are beginning to develop in my lungs.

My legs are growing longer than my arms now, and I can move all of my joints and limbs.

Although my eyes have not opened yet, I can sense light.

I can sense the sunlight. It is amazing. Although I have not seen the sun, I can tell that I will like it.

There's not much for me to taste at this point, but I am forming taste buds and it won't be long now.

Now you can find out whether I am a boy or a girl. But I prefer to keep it a secret.

I love you Mom

Hi baby

Week 16

Hi Mom,

I am about the size of an avocado. Have you noticed how round and voluptuous your body is becoming? As you know, this is a symbol of your fertility and inner beauty.

I have a Great news for you - I am really moving for the first time. My first movements may feel as though you have gas. But it's really me. You might feel some small fluttering movements inside of you. Think about your feelings. Do you feel it? What does this feel like?

Soon you'll start noticing that these movements are becoming more and more frequent and stronger and stronger. It will be a few more weeks before you start feeling kicks and punches.

The patterning of my scalp has begun, though my locks aren't recognizable yet.

My heart is now pumping about 25 quarts of blood each day, and this amount will continue to increase as I continue to grow and develop. As a result you may feel your heart beating 'faster'. This is because there is a lot more blood in your body now. **I love you Mom**

Hi baby

Hi Mom, I can hear you!!!

What a wonderful thing to hear your lovely voice. This is the time when I want you to begin talking to me and singing because I can now recognize your voice.

I'm getting used to familiar sounds, such as the beating of your heart, blood flowing thru your veins, the noise of your intestines. It sounds like the purring of a cat.

I react to sounds and I can turn my head towards a sound. Sharp sounds sometimes frightening me and I cover my face with my hands.

I always hear you when you talk to other people, I can feel your mood and your mood influences my development. And this is very important because it helps in creating my future personality.

I love quiet soft music. I suppose I have inherited that from you. Or from Dad...

Please, for our sake, make sure you are getting the proper amount of sleep and the proper foods.

If you are having trouble finding a comfortable way to sleep, do not sleep on your back.

When you lie on your back, it puts pressure on several important blood vessels. This can decrease circulation to you and to me.

I am about the size of a turnip.

I love you Mom

Hi baby

Week 18

Hi Mom,

I am about the length of a bell pepper.

I can kick, swallow, and sleep.
Also my stomach is developing, so is my intestine and my colon.

My skeleton is changing from soft cartilage to bone, and the umbilical cord is growing stronger and thicker. My sweat glands are starting to develop.

All my sensitivity forms have almost developed already.

This is a period of rapid growth as the fat begins to form underneath my skin.

My tiny heart is pumping as much as 27 quarts of blood a day!
Your heart works almost one and a half times more, than it did before I came along.

I love you Mom

Hi baby

Week 19

Hi Mom,

I am about the size of a large tomato.

My sensory development is exploding! I can even dream (REM sleep)!

My brain has designated specialized areas for smell, taste, hearing, vision, and touch.

Remember - I am able to hear your voice now, so don't be shy about reading aloud, talking to me, or singing a happy song when the mood strikes you.

My arms and legs are in the right proportions to each other and with the rest of my body.

My kidneys are continuing to make urine and the hair on my scalp is beginning to show thru.

A waxy protective coating is forming on my skin to prevent it from pickling in the fluid of my ocean.

I love you Mom

Hi baby

Week 20

Hi Mom,

Now I am about size of a a banana.

I am growing fast and big enough that you should be feeling fluttering or quickening quite regularly now.

In fact, from my movements you may be able to tell if I'm awake or asleep.

I have my favorite sleep position already. I like to sleep with my chin resting on my chest.

I am swallowing more these days, which is good practice for my digestive system.

I am also producing doo-doo, by-product of digestion. This substance will accumulate in my bowels, and you'll see it in my first soiled diaper :)

I have started to practice breathing motions, even though my lungs are not yet mature enough to breathe enough air to allow me to survive outside your body.

I love you Mom

Hi baby

Week 21

Hi Mom,

I am as long as a carrot.

I am a tiny person with tiny hairs on my head, tiny eyebrows and lids and tiny nails on my fingers.

I can do many interesting things now, such as I can yawn, suck my finger and play with my umbilical cord, and do a somersault.

A white-creamy substance is covering the folds and some other sites of my body.

This greasing will protect my gentle thin skin which is being constantly washed by water.

You may soon feel like I am practicing martial arts as my initial fluttering movements turn
into full-fledged kicks and nudges.

You may also discover a pattern to my activity as you get to know me better.

I love you Mom

Hi baby

Week 22

Hi Mom,

Now I am about the size of a spaghetti squash.

I look like a miniature newborn.

I continue to grow and prepare myself for life in your world.

My lips, eyelids, and eyebrows are becoming more distinct.

My eyes have formed.

My internal systems are developing as are the digestive and reproductive system.

My brain has begun a more rapid growth.

Also my body has developed taste buds and may be able to detect strong flavors in my ocean fluid.

If you could see inside, you might catch me sticking out my tiny tongue for a taste and then grimacing, perhaps you should be more careful about eating spicy foods.

I love you Mom

Hi baby

Week 23

Hi Mom,   Let's dance!

Turn on the radio and let's sway to the music.   With my sense of movement so well developed by now, I can feel it when you are dancing.

And now that I am more than 11 inches long and weighs just over a pound, you may be able to see me squirm underneath your clothes.

Some loud noises are becoming familiar to me now, such as a dog barking or the noise of your vacuum cleaner. These things probably won't bother me when I hear them outside of your stomach.

I   am in an   accelerated growth rate and starting to increase my body fat.

I am now about the size of a large mango. I have   become more and more active, but still I push very softly with my legs.

I continue to swallow small amounts of a surrounding liquid and I pee every hour. Liquid swallowing can cause hiccups, which you may feel when I develop a case of them.

My   body   is   becoming   better proportioned every day, and the bones of the middle ear have begun to harden.

I love you Mom

Hi baby

Week 24

Hi Mom,

I am growing steadily and I have gained about 5 ounces since last week.

I am about the size of an ear of corn.

My body is filling out proportionally and I'll soon start to plump up.

My brain is also growing quickly now, and my taste buds are continuing to develop.

My lungs are developing "branches" of the respiratory "tree" as well as cells that produce surfactant, a substance that will help my air sacs inflate when I get to the outside world.

My skin is still thin and translucent, but that will start to change soon.

I don't know yet what the color of my hair will be - a brunette, a blonde, or a redhead?

Actually, right now my hair, such as it is, is white since there's no pigment yet.

I love you Mom

Hi baby

Week 25

Hi Mom,

I am about the size of a rutabaga, but I am beginning to exchange my long, lean look for some baby fat.

My eyes are opening, and I am beginning to see different shapes and forms.

Certainly, here inside of you is not the best place for sight development, but it is enough for a first time.

I see sunlight in muffled orange tones and I react to the sun positively. When the rays are direct I squint my eyes.

I like the sunlight, I can see it thru the clothes you wear.

But I do not need very much sunlight, it makes me tired.

The fingers of my hands are more flexible now. I can even squeeze with either hand.

Every day I become more and more flexible and can already touch my own legs.

When I am awake, I will let you know by my kicks and pushes. You may be feeling like a "Soccer Mom" by now.

I love you Mom

Hi baby

Week 26

Hi Mom,

I am about the size of an English hothouse cucumber.

I am continuing to grow every day and I am putting on more baby fat.

The nerve pathways in my ears are continuing to develop, and this is allowing me to respond to sounds more often.

When there are loud noise, you might notice me jumping more often.

This is a good time to start playing some more relaxing music for me.

For us.

I love you Mom

Hi baby

Week 27

Hi Mom,

Now I am about the size of a head of cauliflower.

I am sleeping and waking at regular intervals, opening and closing my eyes, and sucking my fingers.

My brain is very active now because every day more brain tissue is developing.

Even though my lungs are still immature they are continuing to develop.

Mom, any tiny rhythmic movements you may be feeling is probably caused by my hiccups, which may be common from now on.

Each episode usually lasts only a few moments, and they don't bother me, so just relax and enjoy the tickle.

Mom you need to eat more because our bodies need an extra 300 to 350 calories each day.

So please, eat a little more but make sure it is the right food that you are eating.

I love you Mom

Hi baby

Week 28

Hi Mom,

I am about the size of a Chinese cabbage.

I can now blink my eyes. It is very interesting to me the things that occur behind the walls of my water house.

Above my eyes I am developing thin short eyelashes. Right now my eyes are blue, but not forever. The color of my eyes will be established some months after my birth.

My brain has already developed crinkles. The weight of my brain is continuing to increase.

I am developing billions of neurons in my brain and adding more body fat in preparation for life in the outside world.

The hair on my head is becoming longer.

I can settle down in your body with my head forward or my legs forward. Don't worry, when the time comes, I will be in the right position.

My muscle tone is gradually improving.

Now my lungs are capable of breathing air.

Talk to me more often Mom, because your voice is so soothing to me.

I love you Mom

Hi baby

Week 29

Hi Mom,

I am now about the size of a butternut squash. I look more like a full-grown baby than a fetus.

Time to begin preparation for a birth!!!

My muscles and lungs are continuing to mature, and my head is growing bigger to make room for my developing brain.

To meet my increasing nutritional demands, you'll need plenty of protein, vitamins C, folic acid, and iron. And because my bones are soaking up lots of calcium, be sure to drink lots of milk.

My immune system is starting to function.

Antibodies, transferred from you to me, will help to protect me from an infection after birth.

My tiny teeth are still hidden in my gums. However already an enamel is forming.

I love you Mom

Hi baby

Week 30

Hi Mom,

I am about the size of a cabbage.

I am getting bigger and beginning to need more room in your stomach.

My eyes are wide open now and my eyesight is continuing to develop.

Now I can open and close my eyes. I am becoming more aware of my surroundings.

I can now distinguish between light and dark and I react to a bright light. My eyes can even follow a light source now, and occasionally they produce tears.

My hair is growing, my whole head is now covered.

Mom, I can now feel it when you touch your belly.

Don't be irritated, if I show a lot of movement about the time you are trying to fall asleep.

Now I can recognize your voice and won't be too long until you will be able to hear my voice.

I love you Mom

Hi baby

Week 31

Hi Mom,

As you can feel I am growing bigger and bigger every day, but I guess I don't have to tell you that.

I have gained more weight and you might even call me chubby. I am about the size of four oranges.

My brain is beginning to develop more rapidly.

Except for my lungs, all of my other organs are fully developed.

My kidneys are working well.

My fingernails now reach to the tips of my fingers.

I can move my head from side to side, and as you can feel I can move my arms and legs quite easily.

I am moving a lot too, and you may have trouble sleeping because of it.

But be happy Mom, because all this moving is a sign that I am active and healthy.

I love you Mom

Hi baby

Week 32

Hi Mom,

Only eight more weeks before I arrive in your world.

Are you sure there is enough room in your belly for me to stay here 8 more weeks?

You're gaining about a pound a week and roughly half of that goes right to my body.

In fact, I'll gain a third to half of my birth weight during the next 8 weeks as I fattens up for survival outside of your stomach.

Weight gain is rapid because the muscles are developing and fat is being collected.

I now have my toenails and fingernails, and the real hair.

My skin is becoming soft and smooth as I plump up in preparation for birth.

My skin looks more transparent, less wrinkly and is becoming pinkish in color.

I am starting to look more and more like a real baby should look and I am smiling.

My brain and nervous system are well developed by now.

Now I am beginning to show sensitivity to temperature.

I love you Mom

Hi baby

Week 33

Hi Mom,

I am about the size of a pineapple.

We are one more week closer to the Big day!

My development is totally complete now.

There will not be many changes occurring during this week.

Any further growth and development will be directed toward survival in the outside world.

I am rapidly losing that wrinkled, alien look and my skeleton is hardening.

The bones in my skull aren't fused together, which allows them to move and slightly overlap, and this will make it easier for me to fit through the birth canal.

These bones don't entirely fuse until early childhood, so they can grow as my brain and other tissue expands during my infancy and childhood.

I love you Mom

Hi baby

Week 34

Hi Mom,

I am still growing. I am gaining more weight and increasing in length. I am about size of a cantaloupe

During this week new muscles will begin to form.

More body fat is developing under my skin. This will help me to withstand the different temperatures in your world when I am born.

The fat acts as an insulator and keeps me warm.

My skin has become smoother than ever.

My central nervous system is maturing, also my lungs are continuing to mature.

The liver has started functioning and I am developing an immunity towards mild infections.

My bones are also becoming stronger.

Just like any newborn I can open my eyes when I am awake and close them when I asleep.

My finger nails have grown and are sharp.

My grasp is more firm now.

During this week I will be moving to your pelvis. It won't be long now. Trust me.

I love you Mom

Hi baby

Week 35

Hi Mom,

I now am about the size of a honeydew melon.

I don't have much room to move around here in my world because I am almost too big.

It's so snug here in your belly, I am not likely to be doing somersaults anymore.

My kidneys are fully developed now, and my liver can process some waste products.

Most of my basic physical development is now complete — I'll spend the next few weeks putting on weight.

My hearing is fully functional, so please Mom, talk to me as offer as you can. It is good for me.

After I am born and I hear your voice I will respond to it.

I love you Mom

Hi baby

Week 36

Hi Mom,

Congratulations Mom!
My time in my world inside of your belly is about over and I can be born at anytime.

By now I am in the head down position and sitting in your pelvic bone. Ready to go.

But while it is not time yet I am still putting on weight — at the rate of about an ounce a day.

I am about the size of a crenshaw melon.

I am shedding most of the downy covering of hair that covered my body as well as the waxy substance that covered and protected my skin during my nine-month ocean bath.

For the next couple of weeks, you may start to become anxious.

Now that you know I can be born anytime. Be prepared. It won't be long.

I am so anxious too Mom.

I love you Mom

Hi baby

Week 37

Hi Mom,

Now I am about the size of a stalk of Swiss chard and becoming rounder and rounder everyday.

I am breathing on my own now and I will be born without any physical or health problems.

The most important development at this stage for you Mom, is my position .

You will be experiencing some pressure in the lower abdominal region.

I will now move and shift with my head down and will rest against the pelvic bone.

I guess you are tired of carrying all of this extra weight around. But once I am born you will see that I am worth all of the the aches and pains you have gone thru.

You probably have had thoughts about becoming a mother and wondering whether or not you will be a good mother.

Relax Mom, for I know you are going to be the best mother in the world. I can just feel it. Don't worry about anything.

If you go into labor now, my lungs will likely be mature enough to fully adjust to life outside your belly.

I love you Mom

Hi baby

Week 38

Hi Mom,

I have really plumped up.

My organs have matured and are now ready for life outside your belly.

I have a firm grasp, which you'll soon be able to test when you hold my hand for the first time!

Wondering what color my eyes will be? You may not be able to tell right away. If I am born with brown eyes, they'll likely stay brown.

If I am born with steel gray or dark blue eyes, they may stay gray or blue or turn green, hazel, or brown by the time I am 9 months old. That's because my irises may gain more pigment in the months after I am born, but they usually won't get "lighter" or bluer.

Mom, right now you should avoid any stress of any kind at all times.

Do you have a name picked out for me yet?

I love you Mom.

Hi baby

Week 39

Hi Mom,

Mom, I am waiting to greet the world!

I am completely ready to be born.

I am preparing myself for the final days inside of your body.

I am continuing to gain weight and my lungs are maturing.

Now I am about the size of a a mini-watermelon.

The outer layers of my skin are sloughing off as new skin forms underneath.

My hands are strong and my knees are pressed to my chin.

My finger nails are fully developed and sometimes I even scratch myself with them.

Now I have become quite an independent human being and as such I can execute all my vital functions.

I love you Mom

Hi baby

Week 40

Hi Mom,

I am a baby. Your baby Mom!
You can now hear my heartbeat!
It's hard to say for sure how big I am. But I am big and ready to live in your world.
You can actually "feel" how impatient I am to get out of your belly!
We are getting close to our due date. Don't expect a peaceful sleep at night.
I cannot sleep ether because I am so excited and anxious to meet you and see all the wonders of my new world.
OK Mom, it is about time for me to join in your world!
Don't panic, everything is going to be OK.
So there is nothing to worry about, just sit back and relax until it starts.
Just remember, your labor day is my labor day too and I will try to be as gentle as I can and avoid hurting you.

I love you Mom.

See you soon

Hi baby,

Hi baby,

Welcome

to life !!!

You were born

__/__/_____

Your name is

_____

I love you!!!

Your Mom